First World War
and Army of Occupation
War Diary
France, Belgium and Germany

4 DIVISION
Divisional Troops
234 Machine Gun Company
13 July 1917 - 28 February 1918

WO95/1472/2

The Naval & Military Press Ltd
www.nmarchive.com
Published in association with The National Archives

Published by

The Naval & Military Press Ltd

Unit 10 Ridgewood Industrial Park,

Uckfield, East Sussex,

TN22 5QE England

Tel: +44 (0) 1825 749494

www.naval-military-press.com

www.nmarchive.com

This diary has been reprinted in facsimile from the original. Any imperfections are inevitably reproduced and the quality may fall short of modern type and cartographic standards.

© **Crown Copyright**
Images reproduced by permission of The National Archives, London, England, 2015.

Contents

Document type	Place/Title	Date From	Date To
Heading	WO95/1492 2		
Heading	4th Division War Diaries 234th M.C. Coy 1917 July-1918 Feb		
War Diary	Harve	13/07/1917	16/07/1917
War Diary	Arras	17/07/1917	25/08/1917
War Diary	Arras-Fampoux	26/08/1917	31/08/1917
War Diary	Arras	01/09/1917	08/09/1917
War Diary	Hendecourt	09/09/1917	18/09/1917
War Diary	Pas En Artois	19/09/1917	20/09/1917
War Diary	Proven	21/09/1917	27/09/1917
War Diary	Near Langemarch	28/09/1917	30/09/1917
War Diary	Vulcan Crossing Nr Langemarck	01/10/1917	04/10/1917
War Diary	Nr Langemarck	11/10/1917	10/11/1917
War Diary	Bridge Junction Elverdinghe	11/10/1917	12/10/1917
War Diary	Proven	13/10/1917	14/10/1917
War Diary	Poperinghe	15/10/1917	18/10/1917
War Diary	Wanquetin	19/10/1917	31/10/1917
War Diary	Arras	01/11/1917	31/01/1918
War Diary	In The Field	01/02/1918	28/02/1918
War Diary	Arras	01/02/1918	28/02/1918

4th Division

War Diaries

234th M.G. Coy. July to Dec 1917

~~Jan 1918~~

1917 July — 1918 FEB

Army Form C. 2118.

WAR DIARY
or
INTELLIGENCE SUMMARY.
(Erase heading not required.)

23rd Machine Gun Coy

Place	Date	Hour	Summary of Events and Information	Remarks and references to Appendices
HAVRE	13/4/17		Disembarked — Animals refreshed — Proceeded to Base Camp. No 1. Sector A.	
"	14/4/17		General cleaning up. Inspector of Kits. Sea offluences etc. Bathing in Sea much appreciated, water warm. Visited Ordnance Stores & drew material not issued in England	
"	15/4/17		Under orders for the line. Left HAVRE 7.30 pm. Entraining completed in good time & in an orderly manner	
	16/4/17	2.30 am	Halted at Buchy. BUCHY for refreshment & watering animals. Passed through ALBERT, MIRAUMONT, BAPAUME & ANCRE valley, very interesting to men who had not been on SOMME Battlefield & who were having their first insight into warfare.	
		11.35 am	Arrived ARRAS met by DM.G.O. of 4th Division, detrained & proceeded to FIFE CAMP. ST. NICHOLAS. All ranks pleased to have finished train journey. Settled comfortably in tents.	

Army Form C. 2118.

WAR DIARY
or
INTELLIGENCE SUMMARY.
(Erase heading not required.)

Instructions regarding War Diaries and Intelligence Summaries are contained in F. S. Regs., Part II. and the Staff Manual respectively. Title pages will be prepared in manuscript.

Place	Date	Hour	Summary of Events and Information	Remarks and references to Appendices
ARRAS	17/4/17		Sections training. Transport improving lines. Got in touch with 47th Divisional Staff, Ordnance & A.S.C. C.O. made tour of trenches with D.M.G.O. thought trenches were generally good. Horses easily found & gun positions excellent. Situation discussed with O.C. 10 & 11th M.G. Coy who are holding the front system. Bathing in swimming baths at ARRAS, good place.	
"	18/4/17 9am		Inspection of Company by G.O.C. 47th Divn. report very satisfactory. General remarked on good rifles, & transport turnout. C.O. reconnoitred Corps line of defence & arranged for gun positions to be taken up, in case of emergency. Two O.R. admitted to hospital with measles. Good Coy would be isolated but at very front succeeding.	
"	19/4/17		Training. Lewis officers went over trenches & Coys line, each gun being allotted its position, & in case of enemy attack could come into action very quickly.	

Army Form C. 2118.

WAR DIARY
or
INTELLIGENCE SUMMARY.
(Erase heading not required.)

Instructions regarding War Diaries and Intelligence Summaries are contained in F. S. Regs., Part II. and the Staff Manual respectively. Title pages will be prepared in manuscript.

Place	Date	Hour	Summary of Events and Information	Remarks and references to Appendices
ARRAS	20/9/17		No: 1 & 2 Sections prepare for trenches, remainder of Company training.	
		3 pm	No 1 Section attached to 10th M.G. Coy for instruction in Trench warfare	
			No 2 " " " 11th " " " " "	
	21/9/17		Officers, N.C.O. & 16.O.R. being distributed among the Four teams of above Coys	
		10.30 pm	2ND LIEUT. D.E. FELL & 1.O.R. wounded of No 1 Section wounded by Medium Trench mortar while on Reason in — shot shot, but Sector not seriously alarmed.	
			No 2 Section reported fairly heavy shelling in their Sector, but no casualties	
	22/9/17		C.O. visits line as usual, quiet day, very hot weather	
			Divisional H.Q. & Coy lines shelled during morning, shelling very erratic & scattered, no casualties in Coy, men ordered to take cover	
	23/9/17		Artillery active on trenches. Dummy attack on German trenches at 10.30 pm necessitated men get slight idea of modern Machine Gun cooperation.	
			Artillery barrage.	
			German put barrage on LONE LANE, RIFLE TRENCH, BAYONET TRENCH etc. at intervals during the night.	
			2ND LIEUT T FELL not taken to No. 19. C.C.S. where he is staying.	

Army Form C. 2118.

WAR DIARY
or
INTELLIGENCE SUMMARY.
(Erase heading not required.)

Instructions regarding War Diaries and Intelligence Summaries are contained in F. S. Regs., Part II. and the Staff Manual respectively. Title pages will be prepared in manuscript.

Place	Date	Hour	Summary of Events and Information	Remarks and references to Appendices
ARRAS	24/7/17		No. 3 Section relieve No. 1 Section who are attached 10th M.G. Coy for instructional tour	
"			No. 4 " " " 2 " " " " 11th M.G. Coy " " "	
"			Hot meal on Section return to camp much appreciated. Men beginning to appreciate they are received rations.	
"			Trench Raid carried out at 10.50 pm as usual.	
"	25/7/17		Situation normal. Trench raid cancelled. Major BADHAM takes over D.M.G.O. duties.	
"	26/7/17		Transport lines moved to Q. 16 d. 95 Ref Sheet 51 c N.W. 1/20000, owing to shelling on 24/7/17. Although safer, the new lines are not much appreciated by transport, but all ranks worked hard erecting shelters & improving it lines in general.	
"			Sections on tour report normal conditions.	
"			Major D.M.G.O. does a complete tour of front line system accompanied by Capt Tudor, reconnoitres the Corps Line & arranges for gun positions for barrage fire, in support of "Raid" taking place tomorrow.	

Army Form C. 2118.

WAR DIARY
or
INTELLIGENCE SUMMARY.
(Erase heading not required.)

Instructions regarding War Diaries and Intelligence Summaries are contained in F. S. Regs., Part II. and the Staff Manual respectively. Title pages will be prepared in manuscript.

Place	Date	Hour	Summary of Events and Information	Remarks and references to Appendices
ARRAS	27/4/17	10 am	No. 1 Section goes to front system to take up gun position near ROEUX WOOD ready for Barrage fire to be opened on HAUSA WOOD. 2 Guns take up position near LANCER LANE ready to fire on enemy communication trenches. All positions safely occupied & guns laid by 2.30 pm. No 4 Section leave trenches & return to camp, having had 3 days instructional tour.	
		3 pm	Artillery & Machine Gun barrage opened. Company was their own guns in barrage fire for first time. Great effort to make it a success, & guns fired splendidly. Thought Artillery barrage of 3 minutes too short & not sufficiently heavy, no. of enemy seen to bolt. Who would have a chance for shrapnel barrage? All guns return to camp after barrage. Sgt Phillips wounded.	
ARRAS	28/4/17	10 am	No 4 Section proceed in 2 Motor lorries to ROECLECOURT and LIGNY ST FROCHEL with 4 guns & necessaries for lunch aircraft work in defence of camps. 1 Officer & 29 O.R. sent, though were very tired after leaving trenches, but left for a little rest on arrival.	

A 5834. Wt. W4973/M687 750,000 8/16 D, D. & L. Ltd. Forms/C.2118/13.

WAR DIARY
or
INTELLIGENCE SUMMARY.

Army Form C. 2118.

Place	Date	Hour	Summary of Events and Information	Remarks and references to Appendices
ARRAS	28/1/17	6 p.m.	Two guns of No 1 Section proceed to CUSP TRENCH for indirect night fire on HAUSA WOOD etc. Guns mounted & laid before dark. Four guns No 2 Section take over position in LANCER LANE K.L. & M Posts from No 11 M.G. Company. Remaining gun placed in isolated post in valley off LANCER LANE. Relief complete at 9.30 p.m. Two guns of No 1 Section occupy permanent position near Triple Lock, taken over from No 10 M.G. Coy & 1 Anti Aircraft position off CEYLON TRENCH. Other four guns occupying temporary position in line, not including those specially sent for "Barrels" etc.	
		7.30 p.m	No 3 Section leave the line & return to FIFE CAMP, having been attached to No 10 M.G. Coy 4 days for instruction. Men very tired on arrival owing to Coy headquarters being such a long distance from line, the also gave long & tiring marches for seeking proceeding to trenches for short barrages, & then returning.	

WAR DIARY
or
INTELLIGENCE SUMMARY.
(Erase heading not required.)

Army Form C. 2118.

Place	Date	Hour	Summary of Events and Information	Remarks and references to Appendices
ARRAS	29/4/17	1.0 am	Alt guns open barrage in support of Raid, very successful affair.	
		5 am	Two guns return to camp after Raid, reported Machine Gun had been firing on them + little shelling. No 2 Section report from LANCER LANE that shortly Barrage opened + Enemy S.O.S went up, their very lights ceased to come from the front line + started from the supports. Enemy retaliation very weak + soon ceased. Quiet day followed.	
		5.30 pm	No 3 Section take up 3 guns for fire night firing mounted before dark	
	30/4/17	1.0 am	Four guns firing from SCARPE VALLEY on various targets from 1 to 3.30 am. Got shelled a little	
		5 am	No 3 Section returned to camp.	
	3/5/17	9 pm	Harassing fire carried out during night by 6 guns in conjunction with artillery (wheel & beam) on enemy tracks etc. chiefly near HAUSA WOOD + DUNGAN WOOD.	

E.G. [signature]
Lt 234th Infantry

WAR DIARY
or
INTELLIGENCE SUMMARY.

Army Form C. 2118.

23 & 7th M.G. Coy

Place	Date	Hour	Summary of Events and Information	Remarks and references to Appendices
ARRAS	1/8/17		Miserably wet day, line fairly quiet. Machine guns carry on with harassing fire. No 3 Section goes to line from its support night raid, did harassing fire on CHALK PIT near HAUSA WOOD.	
"	2/8/17		Still very wet & trenches in bad state, except where duck boards are laid. Sections in line seem to be fairly comfortable in spite of weather.	
		11.30pm	Heavy shelling on our right followed by enemy attack, guns laid on S.O.S. lines & opened fire, nothing serious occurred on Division front.	
"	3/8/17		Still wet, quiet day. New S.O.S. lines arranged. Enemy Machine Gun spotted & silenced by No. 2 Section in early morning.	
"	4/8/17		Artillery activity below normal, no Machine Gun firing carried out, owing to Infantry report that state had been telling our own target wire, decided to move at once not the Company. No. 3 & 4 Section relieve No. 1 & 2 Sections in the line, relief complete 9.30pm.	
		10.0 10.4pm	Intense bombardment of CARTRIDGE TRENCH carried out by Artillery, all approaches & exits swept by Machine Gun fire. Harassing fire on HAUSA WOOD.	

WAR DIARY
or
INTELLIGENCE SUMMARY.
(Erase heading not required.)

Army Form C. 2118.

Instructions regarding War Diaries and Intelligence Summaries are contained in F. S. Regs., Part II. and the Staff Manual respectively. Title pages will be prepared in manuscript.

Place	Date	Hour	Summary of Events and Information	Remarks and references to Appendices
ARRAS	5/9/17		Two guns of No 3 Section out of for shoots. Usual Harrassing fire carried out. Section offices went front line during fray. Infantry guns reported that guns of the Company are getting nowhere near them.	APC
	6/9/17	2.0 s 2.9 am	Barrage fire on DECRAP WOOD carried out in support of Trench Raid by 17th Div on our left. Harrassing fire on HAUSA WOOD + Support + I 26 c. That 5/2, 8 / covered.	APC
	7/9/17		Harrassing fire as usual, on various points behind enemy line. 4" Durand Sports held, very good show, much appreciated by all ranks	APC
	8/9/17		All arrangements made for "all day" bombardment of enemy lines preparatory to a raid by 12th Division on our right. 12 guns mounted for barrage fire.	APC
	9/9/17	3.30 am	Enemy bombard Chemical Works on our left quickly followed by large bodies party, they manage to reach our line, but are quickly driven out not heavy loss. Guns on left fire on S.O.S. lines Capt our operations toothaced 24 hours. 2nd Lt SMITH, admitted to XVII Corps Rest station with strained ankle	APC

Army Form C. 2118.

WAR DIARY
or
INTELLIGENCE SUMMARY.
(Erase heading not required.)

Instructions regarding War Diaries and Intelligence Summaries are contained in F. S. Regs., Part II. and the Staff Manual respectively. Title pages will be prepared in manuscript.

Place	Date	Hour	Summary of Events and Information	Remarks and references to Appendices
ARRAS	9/8/17		Twelve guns took up position for barrage fire at 6.30 a.m., in support of attack to be carried out by the right flank of 4th Division & the 12th Division on our right. In conjunction with Artillery harassing fire carried out during the whole day on enemy approaches, tracks etc.	AAA
		7.45 p.m.	Zero hour. Rapid fire opened as barrage lines from Zero + 1 to Zero + 5 & intermittent fire maintained from Zero + 5 to Zero + 45 min. Guns were ordered to be prepared to engage any targets presenting themselves in the sector, but enemy were not observed to come out in the open. Lewis guns in forward positions was encountered by our right Battr. and after their fire from & front, parts of the enemy were, our troops decided to return. The 12th Division however were very successful & got a good footing in the enemy front system & captured about 80 prisoners. This will undoubtedly strengthen our position in front of MONCHY & PREUX.	AAA

Army Form C. 2118.

WAR DIARY
or
INTELLIGENCE SUMMARY.
(Erase heading not required.)

Instructions regarding War Diaries and Intelligence
Summaries are contained in F. S. Regs., Part II.
and the Staff Manual respectively. Title pages
will be prepared in manuscript.

Place	Date	Hour	Summary of Events and Information	Remarks and references to Appendices
ARRAS	10/8/17		Usual harassing fire carried out on enemy tracks, roads etc.	AAA
"	11/8/17		Nothing of unusual occurrence to report. Firing as usual	AAA
"	12/8/17		No 1 & 2 Sections relieve No 3 & 4 in front system, men arrive in camp about 11.30 pm, seem to have had a fairly good time in trenches & are very pleased with rations they got when in the trenches	AAA
	13/8/17		11th Brigade carry out a practice tactical advance. Four of Company gunner act in enemy. Quite a successful day, everyone pleased with the scheme.	AAA
	14/8/17		Usual harassing fire on the line. Men in camp clean up in general & several improvements made to camp and terrace rooms etc.	AAA
	15/8/17		Men in Camp training, all got let better during the day at the Divisional baths. Wet day. Heavy artillery fire everywhere North during the evening.	AAA

Army Form C. 2118.

WAR DIARY
or
INTELLIGENCE SUMMARY.
(Erase heading not required.)

Place	Date	Hour	Summary of Events and Information	Remarks and references to Appendices
AREAS	16/8/17		Usual harassing fire carried out	
"	17/8/17		Section out in line, training, inspected by G.S.O.1, 4th Division. Two guns to 3 Selema march to trenches to do barrage fire, not "sleet" to be shelled at 10.30 p.m. Enemy aircraft very active. A.A gun in action from CRUMP TRENCH, quite a number of air fights.	
"	18/8/17	3 am	Two guns under 2/Lt WHITE relieve two guns of No.11 M.G. Coy in ELBOW & SEABOARD TRENCH. Trenches rather badly knocked about. Heavy shelling of RAILWAY EMBANKMENT in M.24.a. Dugout near Coy- aircraft position in CRUMP TRENCH demolished by direct 8-inch shell. Two occupants killed, but Machine gunners only bruised & shaken, but no-one gun equipment etc.	
"	19/8/17		Fairly quiet day. Six guns do barrage & harassing especially at 10.45 – 11.30 pm LANCE & LANG fans shelled a little.	

Army Form C. 2118.

WAR DIARY
or
INTELLIGENCE SUMMARY.
(Erase heading not required.)

Instructions regarding War Diaries and Intelligence Summaries are contained in F. S. Regs., Part II. and the Staff Manual respectively. Title pages will be prepared in manuscript.

Place	Date	Hour	Summary of Events and Information	Remarks and references to Appendices
ARRAS	20/8/17		No 3 & 4 Sections relieve No 1 & 2 at 8 p.m. Relief completed without difficulty. Visual harrassing fire continued	App
"	21/8/17		Aircraft very active, + anti aircraft gun got several targets whenever aviation quiet.	App
"	22/8/17		Four guns of teams sent to ROEUX COURT to act as Anti aircraft guards of ammunition dumps. 2nd Lt Smith rejoined from Hospital.	App
	23/8/17	1.30 am	SEABOARD TRENCH taken Patrolled with Lac Combs (Trench mortars) no casualties in Coupay, 9 gas om fired.	App
	24/8/17		Harrassing fire carried out on HAUSA WOOD, PELVES LANE etc as usual.	App
	25/8/17		M.G. fire on HAUSA, German DUGOUTS near CRISP TRENCH & PELVES LANE in conjunction with Artillery 6500 rounds fired Enemy retaliation NIL. Some movement of germans noticed in the vicinity of TASSAW WOOD, Range suspect for this target to be engaged by Machine guns. 6th for 6 gun with a range of 3500 yds.	App

A.3834 Wt. W.4973/M687 750,000 8/16 D. D. & L. Ltd. Forms/C.2118/13.

Army Form C. 2118.

WAR DIARY
or
INTELLIGENCE SUMMARY.
(Erase heading not required.)

Instructions regarding War Diaries and Intelligence
Summaries are contained in F. S. Regs., Part II.
and the Staff Manual respectively. Title pages
will be prepared in manuscript.

Place	Date	Hour	Summary of Events and Information	Remarks and references to Appendices
ARRAS - ROMPOUX	27/8/17		Day Quiet, very bad weather. Usual harassing fire under difficulties.	App.
	28/8/17	9.30 10.45 pm	Intermittent fire on CYPRUS & CANDY TRENCHES. PELVES LANE, & tracks in I26 B. — 7500 rounds — . Enemy Machine guns active, considerable amount of firing on ROEUX WOOD, & RAILWAY EMBANKMENT H 24 a.	App.
	29/8/17		HAUSA WOOD & BIT LANE sprinkled at intervals with Machine gun fire. Enemy activity much below normal. Shelling only conspicuous by its absence. Trench in tolerable condition, doefute ingenious onslaughts by the "Weather Clerk."	App.
	29/8/17		Harassing fire on HAUSA WOOD & PELVES LANE as usual. Day very quiet. Small body of enemy troops shelled near BOIS du SART. Effect could not be seen. Weather still very windy & wet.	App.
	30/8/17		Usual harassing fire carried out. Two guns in front line relieved.	App.
	31/8/17	5.30 - 5.00 am	Intermittent firing on enemy made tracks etc in conjunction with Artillery. German Artillery show slight activity compared to previous few days.	App.

O. C. Sepp. Stcupt
COMD'G. No. 234 COY. M.G.C.

284
MACHINE GUN COY.
DATE 31/8/17

Army Form C. 2118.

WAR DIARY
or
INTELLIGENCE SUMMARY.
(Erase heading not required.)

VI 3
2nd Machine Gun Bn

Place	Date	Hour	Summary of Events and Information	Remarks and references to Appendices
ARRAS	1/9/17		Usual Harassing fire continued, enemy aeroplane flying low over ENCAMPMENT. H242. Enemy active with Trench Mortars on SCABARD SUPPORT during night. Enemy M.G. active fire on LANEUR LANE spotted on I.25.d.60.95. + so on Pattern from 9 pm to 3 am. Trench mortars, phone noted. Reply started at I.14.a.95.05. + fired on from N.29.a. greatly dispersed. Some hostile fired on during night.	BM
	2/9/17		HAUSA WOOD sprinkled with bullets at irregular intervals. Enemy put light barrage on SEABOARD TRENCH more enemy movement than usual.	BM
	3/9/17	3.00 13.30am	Enemy trade & CHALK PIT barraged in conjunction with artillery. Situation normal & quiet. 15th Divn M.G.O. visits line.	BM
	4/9/17		5000 rounds fired on enemy targets tracks etc. during the night in conjunction with artillery.	BM
	5/9/17		HAUSA WOOD. PEEVEY VILLAGE & LANE harassed at intervals. Enemy T.M.s open active on SEABOARD SUPPORT.	BM
	6/9/17	6pm	Bn Relieved by N.225 M.G. Coy. All men returned to Camp Tiff Camp without annual occurrence.	BM

WAR DIARY
or
INTELLIGENCE SUMMARY.
(Erase heading not required.)

Army Form C. 2118.

Instructions regarding War Diaries and Intelligence Summaries are contained in F. S. Regs., Part II. and the Staff Manual respectively. Title pages will be prepared in manuscript.

Place	Date	Hour	Summary of Events and Information	Remarks and references to Appendices
AREAS	8/9/17	6.30am	Left FIFE CAMP. 9 mile march to No 1 Camp HENDECOURT. Men marched well. 9 were settled in new camp by 12 noon. Found it necessary to build several new huts to make camp comfortable. Weather fine & dry.	GHN
HENDECOURT	9/9/17		Men getting rest, all very pleased with new camp & glad to leave trenches.	GHN
"	10/9/17		Started training, chiefly doing "New Barrage drill" men very interested & seem to pick up the idea very quickly. Cricket games & Football played after 3.30 pm. Inter Section Football League started, great enthusiasm.	GHN
"	11/9/17		Training continued	GHN
"	12/9/17		Company in practice advance over trenches etc with ferry practice.	GHN
"	13/9/17		Training as usual. Staff ride for officers	GHN
	14-15 16-17 18/9/17		Training according to programme. Football in afternoon. League completed.	GHN

Army Form C. 2118.

WAR DIARY
or
INTELLIGENCE SUMMARY.
(Erase heading not required.)

Instructions regarding War Diaries and Intelligence Summaries are contained in F. S. Regs., Part II. and the Staff Manual respectively. Title pages will be prepared in manuscript.

Place	Date	Hour	Summary of Events and Information	Remarks and references to Appendices
HENDECOURT	18/9/17	9am	Left HENDECOURT & marched to PAS EN ARTOIS, arriving at 3.30 pm. via ADINFER, MONCHY, GRENVILLERS, SOUASTRE. Billets quite good, everyone glad to be back among the civilian element again. Beautiful weather still continues.	
PAS EN ARTOIS	19/9/17		Sorting & cleaning Equipment kit etc & preparing for entraining.	
"	20/9/17	9am	Left PAS-EN-ARTOIS & entrained at MONDICOURT proceeding by train to HOPOUTRE SW of POPERINGHE. Both entraining & detraining carried out quickly & orderly, very little trouble with animals. Marched to POMPEY CAMP. PROVEN, arriving at 8.30 pm. Men tired & quickly settled in new hut accommodation good.	
PROVEN	21/9/17		Improving camp & making sanitary arrangements, complete kit & Equipment inspection. Afternoon Games.	
"	22/9/17		Usual parades, continuation of Barrage drill. Finished off Lewis League M.G test. Being trained into 2 Gunners up.	

Army Form C. 2118.

WAR DIARY
or
INTELLIGENCE SUMMARY.

(Erase heading not required.)

Instructions regarding War Diaries and Intelligence Summaries are contained in F. S. Regs., Part II. and the Staff Manual respectively. Title pages will be prepared in manuscript.

Place	Date	Hour	Summary of Events and Information	Remarks and references to Appendices
PROVEN	23/9/17		Weather really glorious but now with every prospect of lasting. Church Parade.	WM
	24th		Got a gun. Wanted men over to be taken over. Pretty sure entire absence of trouble. Quite active spelling fire etc. Probns neater few.	GM
	25th		Usual parades + football in the afternoon. Played a team from the R.A.O. & lost 4-2 goals. Gun been better or fas Measures.	WM
	26th		Parade etc. Preparations made for moving to new ares tomorrow. A new type of lean Canvas Hut made strong 10ft effective.	WM
	27th		Reveille 6am. Transport proceeding by road moved to ELVERDINGHE at 9.30am. Company marched to INTERNATIONAL CORNER entrained thent for ELVERDINGHE. Arrived at 3.45pm. Rested until 10.30 pm + then proceeded to take over position from 5/4th Warm Cays at LANGEMARCK.	GM

WAR DIARY
or
INTELLIGENCE SUMMARY.
(Erase heading not required.)

Army Form C.2118.

Place	Date	Hour	Summary of Events and Information	Remarks and references to Appendices
NEAR LANGEMARCK	28th	11am	Relief completed. No casualties. A thick mist prevailing &	10pm
		9pm	weather very cool. A good deal of shelling going on aircraft rather active. Enemy trenches slightly.	
	29th		Glorious day. Prospected for new Bangs battery are very heavily ploughed with shells. Not a very good one Villages pretty heavily shelled during day & also Cpy HQrs. Sent for Reports were the same and also passed safely. Pte Knight, wounded but remains at duty.	9pm
	30th		Cold, bright day. Rather below normal shelling aeroplanes active. Shelled all positions shelled fairly heavily near AU BON GITE at 11am. Much warmer now. Pte Knight evacuated.	am
		2pm	evacuated	

C.S.M. M°Coll A/P/Sjt 8.30

Army Form C. 2118.

234 MG Coy
Vol 4

WAR DIARY
or
INTELLIGENCE SUMMARY.
(Erase heading not required.)

Instructions regarding War Diaries and Intelligence Summaries are contained in F.S. Regs., Part II. and the Staff Manual respectively. Title pages will be prepared in manuscript.

Place	Date	Hour	Summary of Events and Information	Remarks and references to Appendices
YPRES CROSSING	1/9/17		Weather splendid. Fairly heavy shelling. Slightly above normal amount of wind fire. Coy 8th subjected a more intensive shelling the night. Lt Douglas slightly wounded by shell - remained at duty.	B
Nr LANGEMARCK	2/9/17		Weather fine again. Fairly quiet day. Pte Williams slightly gassed. The SPEENHOEK shelled at intervals from 3pm to 5pm. Our Barrage trenches subjected + enemys approaches covered all ready for tray.	B
	3/9/17		Fairly quiet again. Rather dull morning with some rain. A slight amount of Registration being carried out by German batteries.	B
	4/9/17		They tried fire although a little much. Bgde HQrs were non. 6 am. Reinforcements to the moment on Barrage started. The first enemy Barrage was not seen until 6.5 am and the own were fired on attacking troops. Machine Gun Barrage was put up by O. (48 guns) P (48 guns) + M (48 guns). The first two fired from 6 am to 6.6 am KH latter from 6 am to 6.15 am.	B

WAR DIARY
or
INTELLIGENCE SUMMARY.
(Erase heading not required.)

Army Form C. 2118.

Place	Date	Hour	Summary of Events and Information	Remarks and references to Appendices
LANGEMARCK	4/10/17	6.25	Two sections (No 2 & 4 Section) advanced to rear White House from which they assaulted their final objective.	SB
		7am	Final battle of troops was seen about continued to come along front path until aft 9 am, when the enemy opened a barrage.	SB
		7.30	Enemy pushed at white stone scooped his position at white stone scooped	SB
		8am	Enemy barrage opened considerably, & there was very heavy on the STEENBEEK area principally 7.5 am & 10.5 am Hours.	SB
		9.30	Stretchers arrived now, Lost many wounded coming back	SB
		10am Barrage	Barrage of enemy now coming down on DAVIES ST & LANGEMARCK Road pretty heavy	SB
		1.50	Opened fire in response to S.O.S. signal on proteture barrage	SB
			End. Casualties during day — fairly heavy 5 O/R killed & 10 O/R wounded. Enemy showed fairly quietly all things considered. Running fearfully O.P. battine unbroken.	SB

Army Form C. 2118.

WAR DIARY
or
INTELLIGENCE SUMMARY.

(Erase heading not required.)

Instructions regarding War Diaries and Intelligence Summaries are contained in F. S. Regs., Part II. and the Staff Manual respectively. Title pages will be prepared in manuscript.

Place	Date	Hour	Summary of Events and Information	Remarks and references to Appendices
Nr LANGEMARCK	31/7/17	6am	Weather turn to good, but hair again of a breeze cleaning shortly. Very quiet two own.	AB
		9am	2 few more casualties occurred. 2/Lt Hom whilst wounded + 7 OR wounded. STEENBEEK & Battery trenches shelled with whizz bangs.	52
		3p	Ordered to relieve 11th Coy (one section) in Barrage trench.	J
		4pm	Relief and up to X2 battery. Left troops at 7pm.	
		8.45	Enemy chipped barrage from REITRES FARM to STEENBEEK. Our artillery putting up a new barrage.	BB
			Shelling upon in normal manner. Rather fine rather cramps only few OR casualties. Opened on 7 GS at DOUBLE COTTS in support to original.	
			In reply annul to [illegible]. In no [illegible] nature Indl in the next relieved + turned out trenches and withdrew	
	1/8/17		Coy held L Camp returned to Langford Farm to rest & work cleaning up etc.	BB

Army Form C. 2118.

WAR DIARY
or
INTELLIGENCE SUMMARY.
(Erase heading not required.)

Instructions regarding War Diaries and Intelligence Summaries are contained in F. S. Regs., Part II. and the Staff Manual respectively. Title pages will be prepared in manuscript.

Place	Date	Hour	Summary of Events and Information	Remarks and references to Appendices
			[illegible handwritten entries]	

Army Form C. 2118.

WAR DIARY
or
INTELLIGENCE SUMMARY.
(Erase heading not required.)

Instructions regarding War Diaries and Intelligence Summaries are contained in F. S. Regs., Part II. and the Staff Manual respectively. Title pages will be prepared in manuscript.

Place	Date	Hour	Summary of Events and Information	Remarks and references to Appendices
	8/9	4p	Went & billet at WHITE HOUSE. Spent 9 mile Plateau got at Dickebers	
	9/9	11p	Having again very heavy enemy shelling somewhat less about 11 pm & sent out for shells. No causalities until 16 pt or so death. Shell shot & several men more or less shaken. Temp relieved by 1st R.A. & Lanc. Regt at 5 A.M. to Junction	
BRIDGE JUNCTION	11/9		Finished quiet day & half. Day very quiet at half an hour. Left at Camp from the hour at 8.30am. Pickum Q. very late in arriving owing to bivouacs getting lost had a good sleep & did manage & men. Left at PROVEN towards Irmsytoot. Spent the about 3 quart of an hr there.	
ELVERDINGHE				
	14/9		Rode up to right to Raine towards ELVERDINGHE at 8.30pm. Left at 6.30pm. Reached bivouac. They are although all through all ravines & Cathedral & anxt	

A.S824 W: W4973/M687 750,000 8/16 D. D. & L. Ltd. Forms/C.2118/13

Army Form C. 2118.

WAR DIARY
or
INTELLIGENCE SUMMARY.
(Erase heading not required.)

Instructions regarding War Diaries and Intelligence Summaries are contained in F. S. Regs., Part II. and the Staff Manual respectively. Title pages will be prepared in manuscript.

Place	Date	Hour	Summary of Events and Information	Remarks and references to Appendices
PRUEM	15/11		[illegible handwritten entry]	
	16/11		[illegible handwritten entry referencing PRUM and XVIII Corps]	
DENNINGE	15/11		Moved to DENNINGE. [illegible]	
	16/11		Fine day. [illegible] training carried out	
	17/11		[illegible handwritten entry referencing XVIII Corps]	
	18/11		[illegible] night	
MARQUIS	19/11		Arrived MARQUIS at 10.30 a.m. [illegible]	

Army Form C. 2118.

WAR DIARY
or
INTELLIGENCE SUMMARY.
(Erase heading not required.)

Instructions regarding War Diaries and Intelligence Summaries are contained in F. S. Regs., Part II. and the Staff Manual respectively. Title pages will be prepared in manuscript.

Place	Date	Hour	Summary of Events and Information	Remarks and references to Appendices
MAROEUIL	20/10/17		Quiet day checking for Kit etc. Billets very good indeed	
	21/10/17		Church Parade. Recreation in afternoon	
	22/10/17		Usual Parades. for Drill etc	
	23/10/17		Getting ready for move to ARRAS.	
	24/10/17		Moved back to ARRAS	
	25/10/17		In the line again. MOTCHY & PRIX sectors. Con. parties good. Dugouts good.	
	26/10/17		Enemy Trench mortars on O9b & O2b ween lines engaged with good fire	
	27/10/17		Very quiet day, wealth went too good for us	
	28/10/17		Lgt Sgt BEETLE TRENCH fired in during daylight	
	29/10/17		do.	
	29/10/17		do. Engaged stong point in O9b.	
	30/10/17		Enemy artly more active also Tr Mors on VIMY AVENUE	
	31/10/17		MOTCHY Kelled fairly heavily all day - Reviews quiet	

A 584. Wt. W4973/M687 750,000 8/16 D. D. & L. Ltd. Forms/C2118/13.

WAR DIARY
or
INTELLIGENCE SUMMARY. 2th Machine Gun Coy

Army Form C. 2118.

Vol 5

(Erase heading not required.)

Instructions regarding War Diaries and Intelligence Summaries are contained in F. S. Regs., Part II. and the Staff Manual respectively. Title pages will be prepared in manuscript.

Place	Date	Hour	Summary of Events and Information	Remarks and references to Appendices
ARRAS	1/4/17		Intraactival relief carried out. Usual harassing fire during night on GREEN WORK.	575
"	2/4/17		Posts S of Bottle in O 9 d fired on in conjunction with artillery. 2000 rate fired	575
"	3/4/17		All guns on line tested for quick mounting & laying in case of S.O.S. Results satisfactory. Schedule fired. Quiet as usual.	293
"	4/4/17	2 am	S.O.S. sent up by infantry on right, everything quiet in 20 minute harass.	575
"	5/4/17		Posts in O 9 d fired on during night in conjunction with Artillery	92
"	6/4/17		Strong point in O 9 b fired on during night. 2000 rats. Rate of arrival the Bosche, as much liver much in muddy trenches.	575
			Enemy M.G. played on VINE AVENUE & FORK RESERVE	
"	7/4/17		1000 rounds fired in O 4 c during night. S.O. went on leave, how returning.	575
"	8/4/17		Quiet day, no firing done	92
"	9/4/17	1.40 a	1st Div on right carried out a Raid in DEVILS TRENCH. 10000 rounds fired on I 32 c & d in support of Raid. Enemy shelled a little by many. 2 out shoot practice has been started & enemy samples relief assembly trenches in vicinity Puts dutton relief carried out 4 pm.	575

A7092). Wt. W11819/M1289A 750,000. 1/17. D. D. & L., Ltd. Forms/C2118/14.

WAR DIARY
or
INTELLIGENCE SUMMARY.
(Erase heading not required.)

Army Form C. 2118.

Place	Date	Hour	Summary of Events and Information	Remarks and references to Appendices
ARRAS	10/4/17		6000 rounds fired on Track in O.3.d. during night, enemy appears to have been considerable work in the vicinity of late, large number of tracks have been visible on aeroplane photos	92
"	11/4/17		No firing today. MONCHY shelled with 4.2. at intervals. Engagement last night been made to move forward in case of retirement by enemy, which appears to be possible. Post pushed(?)	93
"	12/4/17		Enemy M.G.s fairly active, otherwise situation normal. Engagements being made for a raid in about a week.	93
"	13/4/17		Enemy bombarded with Gas shells & T.M.s about 7.30 pm, no casualties in Company. 500 rounds fired at E. Aeroplane.	93
"	14/4/17		300 rounds on FOX TRENCH & vicinity from new Battery position. Officer sent to front line to ascertain of Infantry are satisfied as clearance all reported correct.	93
"	15/4/17		Nothing of interest occurred	93

WAR DIARY
or
INTELLIGENCE SUMMARY.
(Erase heading not required.)

Army Form C. 2118.

Place	Date	Hour	Summary of Events and Information	Remarks and references to Appendices
ARRAS	16/4/17	2 a.m.	L.F. carried out small raid on enemy trenches, but did not get any prisoners. 2000 rounds fired in support of above raid.	P3
"	17/4/17		2000 rounds on tracks in sq "03" ard. After attack R.F.A. fire stop unchecked	Do
"	18/4/17		Harassing two sections of the line in preparation for barrage fire.	Do
"	19/4/17	3 p.m.	Bay shot by Artillery M.G. & T.M's. rounds observed along whole front. Enemy put down barrage immediately, seemed very "wobbly" during remainder of day & shelled heavily about 4.30 & 6-45 p.m. Zero hour fixed 3000 rounds in conjunction with bombardment. This Section (M.G.) feeder for Rt. Battery seems dangerously near Enemy barrage line, several shoot sets in position. Very unfortunate all guns (12) ready, had in position for large raid. Regret better moved back 300 yds & free from shell fire.	D3
	20/4/17		Had test flares at 6.20 a.m. 27,500 rounds fired in support. Enemy all killed, so that not many prisoners were caught. Very successful affair. Lots our killed none found. No casualties in Company.	P3

Army Form C. 2118.

WAR DIARY
or
INTELLIGENCE SUMMARY.
(Erase heading not required.)

Instructions regarding War Diaries and Intelligence Summaries are contained in F. S. Regs., Part II. and the Staff Manual respectively. Title pages will be prepared in manuscript.

Place	Date	Hour	Summary of Events and Information	Remarks and references to Appendices
ARRAS	22/4/17		Retaliation by enemy during night consisted mostly , many rounds very correct on right where damage was being done. Good news received from South , very successful attack appears to have taken place . Allied with considerable works. Many prisoners on the front. Maj. SHIPSTER took over command of Bngers. Enemy artillery activity about normal. Barrage put down on FORK EAST RESERVE . Enemy scrap very windy.	RS/
	23/4/17		Aerial honorary fire carried out. Enemy artillery activity an increasing.	RS/
	24/4/17		Enemy very busy E.A. crossed our line several times during the day. Heavy barrage of all calibres fell in support of Brent line at 11 am	RS/
	25/4/17		Harrassmate fires on enemy back etc during night. C.Obby still very active. Capt Tabor returned to U.K. from Establishment	RS/
	26/4/17		Weather in general keeping indicably more active. Wind bend so to be normal considerably all the nest. 22000 rounds green fired on selected targets	RS/
	27/4/17		Situation normal, 16,000 rounds fired O.S. square	RS/

WAR DIARY
or
INTELLIGENCE SUMMARY.

(Erase heading not required.)

Army Form C. 2118.

Place	Date	Hour	Summary of Events and Information	Remarks and references to Appendices
ARRAS	28/4/17		Harassing fire carried out on SANDER TRENCH & O.9.B. during night. 18 M.G. were four guns on I.5,6,7,8 relieved by three guns where four guns of 10th & 11th M.G. Companies in I.1 & 2 R.10, & 10a. Zero Extra positions had been completely demolished by shell a few days previous. Guns now kept in CHATEAU, MONCHY & mounted only in case of S.O.S. New positions chosen & dugouts rounded. Enemy artillery & T.M.s very active all day.	[sig]
	29/4/17		All firing ceased at 5 a.m., complete quiet & no little movement in front of in sector observed to anything the enemy. Enemy artillery still very active. 2nd Welshmen in Bois.	[sig]
	30/4/17		No flying punctuated artillery, judging by enemy activity he seems to be well warned or deciding to take full advantage of our best of firing. Approach to CHATEAU at MONCHY received direct hit. Carried in impossible at present.	[sig]

Army Form C. 2118.

234 M.G. Coy
Vol C

WAR DIARY
or
INTELLIGENCE SUMMARY.
(Erase heading not required.)

Instructions regarding War Diaries and Intelligence
Summaries are contained in F.S. Regs., Part II.
and the Staff Manual respectively. Title pages
will be prepared in manuscript.

Place	Date	Hour	Summary of Events and Information	Remarks and references to Appendices
ARRAS	1/12/17		Distribution of Company as before. No 1 & No 2 Sections in line (8 guns) & No 3 Section in billets at Coy Head quarters in ARRAS. Relief continue to be carried out fairly regularly every 8 days. Transport in lines in BOUQUOY ROAD. Shells for men & animals quite good, approach & harness sheds need good metal, this is being attended to. Considerable improvement needed. Situation in line continues to be fairly active & enemy artillery is very lively. Harassing fire carried on every night in accordance with weekly programmes issued by 2ND Bgd.	
	2/12/17		Harassing fire carried out on Enemy tracks near SANDER & FOX TRENCHES. Hostile aircraft fairly active & M.G's mounted for A.A. work active.	
	3/12/17		16000 rounds fired on tracks in I.32.b. during night. Enemy artillery again active.	
	4/12/17		16000 rounds again fired on tracks	
	5/12/17		Relief carried out as usual. M.G's now active this section relief carried out.	

Army Form C. 2118.

WAR DIARY
or
INTELLIGENCE SUMMARY.
(Erase heading not required.)

Instructions regarding War Diaries and Intelligence Summaries are contained in F. S. Regs., Part II. and the Staff Manual respectively. Title pages will be prepared in manuscript.

Place	Date	Hour	Summary of Events and Information	Remarks and references to Appendices
ARRAS	9/10/17	9.50 p	S.O.S. sent up by Division on right. Two guns rectifying I 14 2 broken on right flank. 3000 rounds in reserve. 1000 rounds fired during night, searching for	
"	6/2/17		Nothing unusual observed	
"	7/8/17		Situation rather more quiet, no firing done. 2nd Lt Yates returned from M.G. Course at CAMIERS. Large numbers of Officers & N.C.O. soon to be required for courses at present, rather upsets the fighting strength of unit.	
	8/8/17		Harrassing fire continued. Rumours seem prevalent that the enemy may attack. Independence for defence commenced.	
	9/9/17		Reserve lines heavily shelled by enemy at intervals during the day	
	10/9/17		Coy's line manned at 7.0 am. Four of the guns in ARRAS sent to take up position there. Emplacements improved & CAM placed in Position. One Section remaining in ARRAS, Cathe hye & Rille at 11.0 am.	

Army Form C. 2118.

WAR DIARY
or
INTELLIGENCE SUMMARY.
(Erase heading not required.)

Instructions regarding War Diaries and Intelligence Summaries are contained in F. S. Regs., Part II. and the Staff Manual respectively. Title pages will be prepared in manuscript.

Place	Date	Hour	Summary of Events and Information	Remarks and references to Appendices
ARRAS	11/2/17		Orders received that, if two Sections of Company in ARRAS, one section would "Stand to" daily at 6.30 am & be prepared to proceed on receipt of orders to take up position on CORPS LINE. "Stand down" being ordered each day by O.C Division, as soon as the situation appeared clear.	B
	12/2/17		Preparation for Enemy attack continued. Weather becoming rather cold, trench feet precautions necessary. Enemy dropped Gas shells in MONCHY & vicinity, seems to be a very new type of gas with sulphurous acidy smell. C.O. slightly affected whilst nearing position, otherwise no damage.	B
	13/2/17		Shrapnel relief carried out. 3000 rounds fired on enemy trenches.	B
	14/2/17		More gas shells west of enemy.	B
	15/2/17		"Stand to" still continued in ARRAS. Weather still continued cold. Thermometer for 20 cold.	B

A7092I. Wt. W11819/M1492. 750,000. 1/17. D. D & L., Ltd. Forms/C2118/14.

Army Form C. 2118.

WAR DIARY
or
INTELLIGENCE SUMMARY.
(Erase heading not required.)

Instructions regarding War Diaries and Intelligence Summaries are contained in F. S. Regs., Part II. and the Staff Manual respectively. Title pages will be prepared in manuscript.

Place	Date	Hour	Summary of Events and Information	Remarks and references to Appendices
ARRAS	16/10/17		Situation normal, heavy fire as usual	
	17/			
	18/			
	19/			
	20/10/17		Enemy attempted a raid on Devt front, which was slightly unsuccessful, failed to reach our wire	
	21/10/17			
	22/10/17		NIL	
	23/10/17	6.25pm	Another raid attempted by enemy, all guns opened fire on S.O.S. lines, & appear to have taken a few prisoners	
			Situation quiet	
	24/10/17		"Stand to" in ARRAS at 6.30 am daily, cancelled	
	25/10/17			
	26/			
	27/			
	28/			
	29/			
	30/10/17		Nothing unusual, beyond the ordinary trench routine.	

S.E.Bayntun Capt
O.C. 234th Tr. 9 Coy

Army Form C. 2118.

WAR DIARY
or
INTELLIGENCE SUMMARY.
(Erase heading not required.)

Instructions regarding War Diaries and Intelligence Summaries are contained in F. S. Regs., Part II. and the Staff Manual respectively. Title pages will be prepared in manuscript.

33rd M.G.[?] Bn

Place	Date	Hour	Summary of Events and Information	Remarks and references to Appendices
ARRAS	1/1/18		Disposition of Company as follows:—	
		8 a.m.	B Reserve & Intermediate line in MONCHY & PRUOX Sector.	
		8 a.m.	C & D Reserve in billet at ARRAS. Company Headquarters at ARRAS. Transport lines at RONVILLE just outside ARRAS. Nothing of unusual occurrence taking place to mark the new year except that enemy artillery seem fairly active about the time of their new year. The compliment being returned by "ourselves" about midnight. 4000 rounds fired on enemy tracks etc during the night	⊕
"	2/1/18		Had a practice "stand to" for sections in reserve, result very satisfactory, ready to move 40 minutes after order was received, little led weather for moving transport. Usual firing continued	⊕
"	3/1/18		Enemy artillery rather more active than usual during night	⊕
"	4/1/18		Retaliatory fire as usual, Monchy shelled rather heavily with HE & gas at 9.45 p.m. Hostile M.G. more active than usual.	⊕

Army Form C. 2118.

WAR DIARY
or
INTELLIGENCE SUMMARY.
(Erase heading not required.)

Instructions regarding War Diaries and Intelligence
Summaries are contained in F. S. Regs., Part II.
and the Staff Manual respectively. Title pages
will be prepared in manuscript.

Place	Date	Hour	Summary of Events and Information	Remarks and references to Appendices
ARRAS	5/1/18		Election normal.	GB
	6/1/18		Inter Coln relief carried out. Two guns from Billets ordered to take up positions in CORPS "LINE" to relieve 12" M.G. Coy. Usual harassing fire carried out. Very cold weather just now. Little snow about. D.M.G.O. went on Course & CMM1EPS	
	7/1/18		Major SHIPSTER now acting D.M.G.O. Considerable work on hand preparing new Defence Scheme. Several new M.G. emplacements under construction.	GB
	8/1/18		Situation extremely fairly quiet. Harassing fire carried out each night on new track enemy is making at I32 & Y2.	GB
	9/1/18		Front continues, nothing unusual to report.	GB
	10/1/18		All guns take up new positions, the new system of M.G. defense comes into operation at 5.0 p.m. Not many of the new dugouts are yet completed but accommodation has been found for men in various dugouts in vicinity. From new trenches all guns are mounted at night & laid on S.O.S. lines for can therefore be opened on a few seconds after S.O.S. signal is given.	GB

A.F.G. Wt. W128.9/M1293. 750,000 1/17. D.D & I. Ltd. Forms/C2118/14.

Army Form C. 2118.

WAR DIARY
or
INTELLIGENCE SUMMARY.
(Erase heading not required.)

Instructions regarding War Diaries and Intelligence Summaries are contained in F. S. Regs., Part II. and the Staff Manual respectively. Title pages will be prepared in manuscript.

Place	Date	Hour	Summary of Events and Information	Remarks and references to Appendices
ARRAS	12/1/18		Very little firing done at night now, owing to gunn teams registered in their SOS lines. Two Sections of Company in ARRAS prepared to move forward at moments notice. Great preparations to secure the Bridge of the canal over Fivesst portion of gun 4 on MONCHY, 4 in nests S. of MONCHY.	B
"	13/1/18			B
	13/1/18 4.45pm	Enemy attempted to raid our trenches, seems to have been stopped at the wire. M.G. response at S.O.S. very satisfactory, Raid stopped by M.G. & rifle fire (see Early report). Enemy very active with Trench Mortars.	B
	14/1/18		Situation quiet. Few shells on MONCHY & vicinity. Otherwise all quiet.	B
	15/1/18		No firing done now, all quiet	B
	16/1/18 17/1/18 18/1/18 19/1/18		Everything normal. Trenches in very bad state, thaw having started & large quantities of rain fallen. Most trenches quite impassable	B

Army Form C. 2118.

WAR DIARY
or
INTELLIGENCE SUMMARY.
(Erase heading not required.)

Instructions regarding War Diaries and Intelligence Summaries are contained in F. S. Regs., Part II. and the Staff Manual respectively. Title pages will be prepared in manuscript.

Place	Date	Hour	Summary of Events and Information	Remarks and references to Appendices
ARRAS	20/1/18		Great local activity, otherwise very little occurring with exception of mud.	
	21/1/18		Weather precaution in force. Great care taken to prevent trench feet. Relieve have to be used in Post arrivals now.	
	22/1/18		Ordr. section reliefs carried out	
	23/1/18		Roads & trenches now improving. All quiet in line	
	24/1/18		Company conducted short of officers, owing to Courses etc.	
	25/1/18		Enemy artillery seems to be necessary in activity, possibly due to thaw & relief. Shells most annoying to working parties & men who continue to use without roads owing to bad trenches.	
	26/1/18		Artillery still fairly active, but rumours of coming relief make the men quite interesting for the time being	
	27/1/18		NIL	

A 7092 Wt. W 1128 g/M 1293 750,000. 1/17. D. D & L. Ltd. Forms/C 2118/11.

Army Form C. 2118.

WAR DIARY
or
INTELLIGENCE SUMMARY.

(Erase heading not required.)

Instructions regarding War Diaries and Intelligence Summaries are contained in F. S. Regs., Part II. and the Staff Manual respectively. Title pages will be prepared in manuscript.

Place	Date	Hour	Summary of Events and Information	Remarks and references to Appendices
ARRAS	28/1/18	2.50am	10 minute bombardment by enemy. nothing serious developed	
	29/1/18		Enemy attempted raid on Divn on our left, none of the Company did not fire.	
	30/1/18		Sector very quiet.	
	31/1/18		do.	

Stephenson Capt
COMDG No. 284 COY. M.G.C.

Army Form C. 2118.

WAR DIARY
or
INTELLIGENCE SUMMARY.
(Erase heading not required.)

Instructions regarding War Diaries and Intelligence Summaries are contained in F. S. Regs., Part II. and the Staff Manual respectively. Title pages will be prepared in manuscript.

Place	Date	Hour	Summary of Events and Information	Remarks and references to Appendices
In the Field	1/2/18		FRANCE:— MAPS REFERENCE Sheet 51B. S.W. } 1/20,000 " 51B. N.W. } On this date the Company was in the line & situated as follows:— Company HQ at N.4 & 9.5 No 2 Section in CORPS LINE " 1 " 1 Gun at H.36.a. 50. 55. " " 1 " " H.36.a. 00. 33 " " 1 " " H.36.a. 25. 03 " " 1 " " H.36.c. 35. 6 " 3 Section 1 " " Z.31.c. 47. 02 " " 1 " " H.36.d. 15. 65. " " 1 " " H.36.K. 63. 30 " 4 Section 1 " " N.6.a. 88. 63 " " 1 " " N.6.a. 22. 41 " " 1 " " H.36.c. 45. 25. " " 1 " " H.36.c. 11. 71. At 10.15 PM the enemy put down a heavy barrage on our trenches, and all Machine Guns fired on their S.O.S. lines until the situation was again quiet.	1 O.R. leave to U.K

Army Form C. 2118.

WAR DIARY
or
INTELLIGENCE SUMMARY.
(Erase heading not required.)

Instructions regarding War Diaries and Intelligence Summaries are contained in F. S. Regs., Part II. and the Staff Manual respectively. Title pages will be prepared in manuscript.

Place	Date	Hour	Summary of Events and Information	Remarks and references to Appendices
In the Field	2/2/18		At 8.30 A.M. the Brigade on our right raided the enemy's trenches. Two Machine Guns under 2nd Lt FRAYLING were in position at O.9.a.3.6 and fired for twenty minutes on hostile M.G. emplacements at O.9.a.15.90. 6000 rounds per gun were expended	
"	3rd		This day was very quiet and Machine Guns did no harassing fire	
"	4th		Usual trench routine; no harassing fire was carried out.	
"	5th		On this date the Company was relieved by the 45th M.G. Coy. & one section of the 225th M.G. Coy. On completion of relief the Company moved to billets in ARRAS.	
"	6th		The morning was spent in cleaning guns and gear, clothing spare parts & & c.	

ARRIVALS
- 1 O.R. from leave.
- Sgt Hughes from M.G. Course
- 2 O.Rs from hospital

DEPARTURES
- 1 O.R. to hospital
- 1 O.R. to U.K.
2nd Lt LABES to I.O.R. (Ileccourt?) to R.F.C. R.A. Course.

Army Form C. 2118.

WAR DIARY
or
INTELLIGENCE SUMMARY.
(Erase heading not required.)

Instructions regarding War Diaries and Intelligence Summaries are contained in F. S. Regs., Part II. and the Staff Manual respectively. Title pages will be prepared in manuscript.

Place	Date	Hour	Summary of Events and Information	Arrivals	Departures	Remarks and references to Appendices
Etaples	7th		From 9AM to 1PM the company route marched. A foot inspection occupied the afternoon.	1 O.R. from hosp.		
"	8th		The day was spent as follows :- 9AM to 1PM Route march 3PM Foot inspection.	1 O.R. from hosp.		
"	9th		The company paraded at 8AM and marched to the short M.G. range, where table C, part 1, was fired. From 2.30PM to 4PM the company were at the baths at SCHRAMM BARRACKS.	2nd LABES 1 O.R. (on Summary) Team R.F.C. Course 1 O.R. from Hospital	1 O.R. to CCS 1 O.R. to Hospital	
"	10th		The morning was spent in Church Parade, the remainder of the day being a holiday.	1 O.R. from team	Lt. Hanson to M.G. Course Captain, 2nd Lt. BES 1 O.R. (on Summary)	to P.B.T. Course
"	11th		The company, with transport, paraded at 9.30AM and marched to new billets in SCHRAMM BARRACKS, and became a company in the Divisional Machine Gun Battalion.		1 O.R. home to UK	

Army Form C. 2118.

WAR DIARY
or
INTELLIGENCE SUMMARY.
(Erase heading not required.)

Instructions regarding War Diaries and Intelligence Summaries are contained in F. S. Regs., Part II. and the Staff Manual respectively. Title pages will be prepared in manuscript.

Place	Date	Hour	Summary of Events and Information	Remarks and references to Appendices
In the Field	12/2/18		The following parades were carried out:- 9 A.M. Inspection. 10.30 A.M. Company drill under C.S.M. 11.30 A.M. Wickmism under Section Officers	
"	13th		The company carried out the following parades:- 8.30 A.M. March to parade ground. Infantry drill under R.S.M. 10.30 AM to 11.15 AM Physical Training 11.30 AM to 12.15 PM T.O.E.T. Four N.C.Os paraded under the R.S.M. from 2 PM to 2.45 PM.	
"	14th		The day was spent as follows:- 8.45 A.M. March to parade ground for Physical Training. 10.30 A.M. T.O.E.T. 11.30 A.M. Wickmism.	
"	15th		The company paraded for work as under:- 8.45 AM March to parade ground for drill under R.S.M. 10.30 AM to 11.15 AM T.O.E.T 11.30 AM to 12.15 PM Wickmism 1.30 P.M. Scrubbing of equipment.	

ARRIVALS:
1 O.R. from shops
2nd Lt INSIPP 3.O.R. from XVII Corps W/ Course
2 O.R. Runf/s from Hoof to Brine Battalion
Lt WILLOUGHBY from leave

DEPARTURES:
Lgt Harris to Brine for Business
Col Myniter Lieut G Conner lawyers

WAR DIARY
or
INTELLIGENCE SUMMARY.

(Erase heading not required.)

Army Form C. 2118.

Place	Date	Hour	Summary of Events and Information			Remarks and references to Appendices
				ARRIVALS	DEPARTURES	
Sulva	16/7/18		The following parade was carried out:- 8.45 A.M. March to parade ground. 9.10 A.M. to 10.10 A.M. Physical Training. 10.30 A.M. to 11.15 A.M. Drill under R.S.M. 11.30 A.M. to 12.30 P.M. I.A. under section officers. 2 P.M. cleaning equipment.			
"	17th		The morning was spent in church parade. At 12 noon the company paraded + were entertained to the "1914 Star" had the ribbon presented to them by Lieut Colonel Somerville, commanding 4th Batt M.G. Corps.	I.O.R. from leave	I.O.R. to Hosp.	
"	18th		The company paraded at 9 A.M. in full marching order for a route march, billets were not reached until 3 P.M.			
"	19th		The day was spent as follows:- 9 A.M. March to parade ground. 9.15 A.M. to 11.15 A.M. drill with pack animals. 10.30 A.M. to 12.15 P.M. drill under R.S.M. 2 P.M. to 2.45 P.M. I.A.	1 Rank and File posted to 10th F Am.B. 1 Rank and File transfered to 11th F Am.B.		

Army Form C. 2118.

WAR DIARY
or
INTELLIGENCE SUMMARY.
(Erase heading not required.)

Place	Date	Hour	Summary of Events and Information	Arrivals	Departures	Remarks and references to Appendices
Bus ies Artois	20th /3/16		While stations of the company, co-operated with the 1st Infantry Brigade in a Ground Scheme. The parade at 6.30AM & marched to Warley field firing range. The fourth action service was the usual funster.		1. O.R. to Hosp.	
"	21st		The following parade were carried out:— 7.45 AM March to funster ground. 9.15 AM to 10.15 AM. Battalion will under R.S.M. 10.30 AM to 11.15 AM. T.O.E.T. 11.30 AM to 12.15 PM Musketry 1.45 PM to 3 PM Testing of Box Respirators by Divisional Gas Officer.		1. OR to Hosp. 1 OR Barrack.	
"	22nd		The company carried through the following programme:— 8.45 AM March to parade ground. 9.15 AM to 10.15 AM. Section from numbers. 10.30 AM to 11.15 PM. T.O.E.T. 2 PM to 2.45 PM Lecture on Snipers Fire	Major Pearse & 2/Lt IV Commander E Routh 2/Lt W Patter 10.55 PM Major Bennet 2.02 PM 46 O.R. 2 OR from Hosp	Departures 1.0 R to Hosp.	
"	23rd		The morning was spent on the 30 yards range, when Lieut G. Peck I was spirit. When returning to billets, men were chewed & held fielded in the afternoon. Firer proficient was most carried out.	2.03 PM from Hosp 5 OR to Hosp 1 OR Barrack		

Army Form C. 2118.

WAR DIARY
or
INTELLIGENCE SUMMARY.
(Erase heading not required.)

Instructions regarding War Diaries and Intelligence Summaries are contained in F. S. Regs., Part II. and the Staff Manual respectively. Title pages will be prepared in manuscript.

Place	Date	Hour	Summary of Events and Information	Remarks and references to Appendices
Busseboom	24/2/18		The day was spent in Church Parades & thorough overhaul of kits.	
	25th		The morning was spent as follows:— 9.15 A.M. – 10.45 A.M. Barrage Drill. 11 A.M. – 11.45 A.M. Sighting & laying. 12 Noon – 12.30 P.M. Preparing guns for range. The My. Guns were sent on Waltz range, where Take 'C' Part II was fired.	
	26th		The following parades were carried out:— 9.15 to 10.15 A.M. Indicator & Recognizer. 10.30 to 11.15 A.M. Sight setting & Laying. 11.30 A.M. & 12-10 P.M. Effect firing Section. 2 P.M. to 2.45 P.M. Lecture & Musketry in Barrage. During the morning the Lewis guns were fired at then find were @ hour 1 & the short range. The afternoon was spent in cleaning guns, just fitting & a kit inspection.	1 ORF. an r/Tagoo. 2 ORF. from 1/Yorks/Public 1. OR to damp. (Attached) 1. OR from damp.
	27th			1OR from transit Lft. Mt. Gritton Base Depot. 1.OR from damp.
	28th		The following parades were carried out:— 9.15 to 10 A.M. Physical Training. 10.15 AM to 12.15 P.M. Section Drill 2. P.M. up 3 to 5 P.M. Musketry	3 OR from trans depot. 1 OR to damp

WAR DIARY or INTELLIGENCE SUMMARY

Army Form C. 2118.

234 M.G. Coy

Place	Date	Hour	Summary of Events and Information	Remarks and references to Appendices
ARRAS	1/4/18		Disposition of Company as follows: 8 guns in line, 8 guns in reserve at ARRAS.	
	2/4/18	10.40pm	Enemy put down heavy barrage on front, rifle fire & 6000 rounds fired in S.O.S. lines.	
			2nd Lt Wellington M.G. carried out a very successful raid on enemy trenches. Was out till shortly before dawn & brought back information & killed several Germans & helped several of the enemy. 15000 rounds fired in support of raid.	
	3/4/18		Enemy shelling fairly active.	
	4/4/18		Quiet	
	5/4/18		Four guns relieved by No 45 (M) Coy.	
	6/4/18		Remaining 4 guns relieved by 45 M.G. Coy & Coy moved to billets in ARRAS.	
	7/4/18		Cleaning & training & reorganisation. Coy rested from the line.	

WAR DIARY
or
INTELLIGENCE SUMMARY.
(Erase heading not required.)

Army Form C. 2118.

Place	Date	Hour	Summary of Events and Information	Remarks and references to Appendices
ARRAS	11/9/7		Company to be ready to take over front of line on short notice preparatory and according	
	12			
	13			
	14			
	15		Training	
	16/9/17			
	17/9/17		Company moved to SCHRAM BARRACKS Hall M.S. Camp 157 m Division now billeted together preparatory to further of theatre	
			Hand Grenade Instruction	

www.ingramcontent.com/pod-product-compliance
Lightning Source LLC
Chambersburg PA
CBHW081425200426
R18166900001B/R181669PG43193CBX00002B/3